The Elders' Colony

Raúl Figueroa-Rodríguez

The Elders' Colony

ISBN-13: 978-1494478698

ISBN-10: 1494478692

To my wife Idania for all the support and help.

Table of Contents

Introduction

Puerto Rico is one of the most beautiful countries in the world. The tropical island has gorgeous beaches, friendly people, and delicious food. In other words, this small country located in the Caribbean is a vacationer's paradise. Given these positive attributes, why are so many people leaving Puerto Rico to live in the United States? Why are they willing to abandon the tropical weather and beauty of the island? Why move to the United States instead of a country with Spanish as its main language? What is going to be the future of Puerto Rico if the exodus continues? The answers to these questions are the groundwork for this book.

This book is about demography. More specifically, it is about the demography of one of the oldest colonies. Puerto Rico, after all, is a territory that for centuries has been unable to chart its own destiny or make its own choices. It's an area where people go to war without the right to vote for their Commander in Chief, in this case, the President of the United States. The fact that Puerto Rico is a colony cannot be ignored; therefore, the implications to demography are essential components of this publication.

Puerto Rico had been a colony of the United States since 1898, and before that was a colony of Spain. Some people prefer calling the current political status of Puerto Rico as an unincorporated territory, or a Commonwealth which is the official name. Others fail to acknowledge that Puerto Rico is under a colonial situation, even when the United States

Supreme Court declared that: "Puerto Rico belongs to, but is not part of the United States."[1]

Puerto Rico is neither an independent nation nor a state. However, the current colonial status grants Puerto Ricans some crucial benefits such as the United States citizenship; but it's a pared down citizenship that exposes the colonial status of Puerto Rico. It's a citizenship that denies Puerto Ricans a proper representation in the United States Congress. For a Puerto Rican, the only way to get all the privileges, rights and responsibilities, is to migrate to one of the 50 states on the nation.

The ease with which Puerto Ricans can travel to the United States is essential for this discussion. For Puerto Ricans, traveling to the United States is cheap, with no passport or visa required. Traveling to Puerto Rico is like traveling to any other state, the main differences are the tropical weather and the language. That makes it very easy for Puerto Ricans to emigrate when needed; something that is becoming more common in recent years.

There is a noticeable contrast between the demographic characteristics of the residents of Puerto Rico and that of the residents of the 50 states of the nation. Most of the socioeconomic characteristics of Puerto Rico make the states look like a paradise to live in. The statistics do not lie. The island ranks high in areas such as homicides, unemployment, poverty, and other significant but negative indicators. Puerto Rico is a

---

[1] Downes v. Bidwell, 182 U.S. 244, 287 (1901).

colony with demographic characteristics of a developed nation, but with an economy of a developing country.

The political status has been one of the central problems in Puerto Rico. Another problem has been the lack of knowledge of the structure and dynamics of the population, and its relationship with the economy, the environment, and other aspects of society. The latter promoted ineffective policies and detrimental decisions. Most of the time, these decisions had a high cost to society and the economy.

In this book, the main demographic topics are described in a style that is easy to understand. The target of the book is the general population. I wanted to make this book useful for policy-makers, business people, or anyone interested in the demographic future of Puerto Rico. Since Puerto Rico is neither a state, nor a sovereign country, I will make comparisons with both, other foreign countries and with the states of the nation. The first chapters of the book include the reasons for the population decline in Puerto Rico and the role of colonialism in the demographic changes. These chapters covered the exodus of Puerto Ricans to the United States, the reason for the mass emigration, and changes in births and mortality patterns. In the next chapters, I presented information related to the aging of the population and its implications, especially to the economy. Additionally, I describe the challenges and opportunities that come with the aging of the population, and explain what Puerto Rico will experience, if there is not a plan to address these challenges.

One-way Ticket

Puerto Rico's population is shrinking. According to the 2010 Census data, Puerto Rico lost population for the first time since its inclusion to the decennial Census program, in the year 1910. The population decreased from 3.8 million residents in the year 2000 to 3.72 million residents in the year 2010[2], which represents 2.2% of the population (Figure 1). The decrease in the population was a surprise for many people who anticipated an increase as observed in past censuses. Additionally, the population fell short from the projection of nearly 4 million people. As expected for something that breaks the prevailing trend, the decline of the population was difficult to accept, especially for mayors and other policy-makers.

The main reason for the downfall of the population has been the exodus of Puerto Ricans to other countries, mainly the United States. The situation of Puerto Rico reached a level that, for some people, an airplane ticket was their only hope for a better future. Thousands of people were forced, sometimes against their will, to abandon their country with expectations of finding a better place to live. These were citizens looking for a more stable and less violent community. They were looking forward to a place with a decent job and better education for their children, as well as far from the constant flow of bad news in the

---

[2] United States Census Bureau / American FactFinder. "QT-P1: Age groups and sex: 2010." 2010 Census. U.S. Census Bureau, 2010. Retrieved from http://factfinder2.census.gov

media. Listening to the local radio or reading the news could have been enough motivation to leave the country in many cases.

Figure 1. Population of Puerto Rico, 1910 to 2010

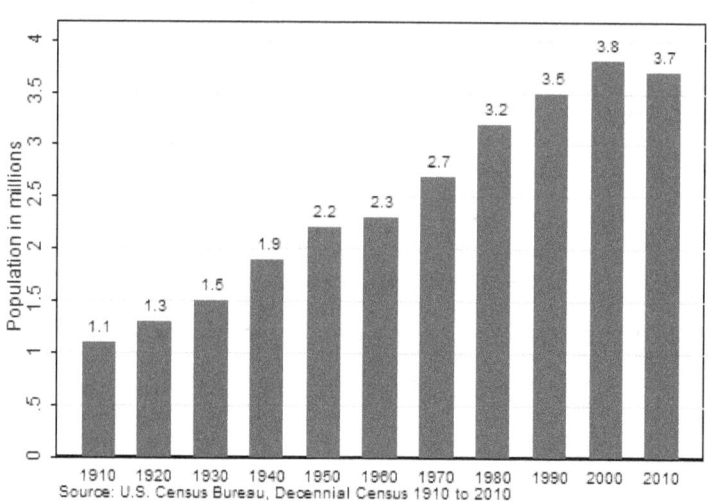

Sometimes Puerto Ricans migrating to the United States became the target of attack by people who did not understand the migration dynamics. Emigrants have been called cowards or traitors for taking the "easiest" way out of their problems in Puerto Rico. The people leaving the island have been asked, by various government administrations, to stick around, embrace their patriotism and wait for the "bright" future they promised. The people who are accusing migrants of giving up on their country, fail to acknowledge that faith and promises do not bring food to the table or a family member back from being a murder victim.

Politicians do not realize that the choices they made contributed to the emigration of Puerto Ricans for decades. Puerto Ricans have been driven out of the country by decades of questionable legislation and decisions.

These decisions have been affecting the population growth by influencing the economic environment, the cost of living, and the quality of the services provided by the government. Additionally, these decisions have led to fewer jobs, more violence, and broken social protection systems.

It is not a surprise that thousands of Puerto Ricans decided to abandon their country each year. In 2012, there were more people of Puerto Rican origin living in the United States (4.9 million) than in Puerto Rico (3.5 million). The current colonial status allows Puerto Ricans to board an airplane and move to the United States. It is easy to abandon the country; that is why for the last 11 decades the net migration has been negative on the island of Puerto Rico (Figure 2). In other words, the numbers of people who leave Puerto Rico outnumber the ones who enter it with the intention to settle down on the island. Once the negative net migration outnumbered the natural growth of the population in the year 2004, the population began to decrease. To this date, the population continues to decline and at a faster pace (Figure 3).

The most troubling issue with the exodus during the past few years has been the characteristics of the emigrants. Especially disconcerting has been the number of young people abandoning the country. According to the Migrants Profile by the Puerto Rico Institute of Statistics[3], the median age of the emigrants for the year 2011 was 29.2 years of age. That was 8.2 years below the median age of the general population in

---

[3] Rodriguez-Ayuso, I. R.; Geerman, K; Marazzi-Santiago, M. (2012). Perfil del Migrante, 2011 [Migrants Profile, 2011]. San Juan, Puerto Rico. Obtenido de www.estadisticas.gobierno.pr

Puerto Rico (37.4 years). Furthermore, 27.7% of the people who emi-
grated had between 18 and 29 years of age. This is a high percentage
when compared to the 16.6% of people between this age group who
resided on the island in that year. During the past decade, Puerto Rico
gave up people in their more productive years to other nations, hurting
the economy and speeding up the aging of the population. Without a
doubt, the recent mass emigration has been the most dangerous aspect for
the economy.

Figure 2. Net migration of Puerto Rico, 1900 to 2010

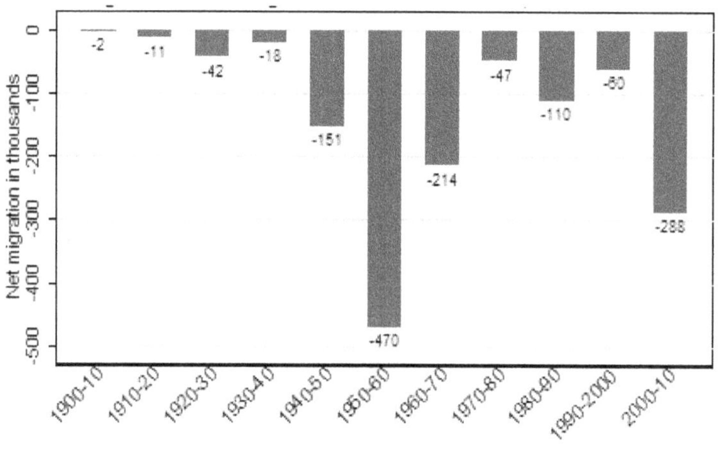

Source: Vázquez Calzada, J.L. (1988). La población de Puerto Rico y su trayectoria
histórica p. 286 and Puerto Rico Planning Board

Figure 3. Population estimates, Puerto Rico 2000 to 2012

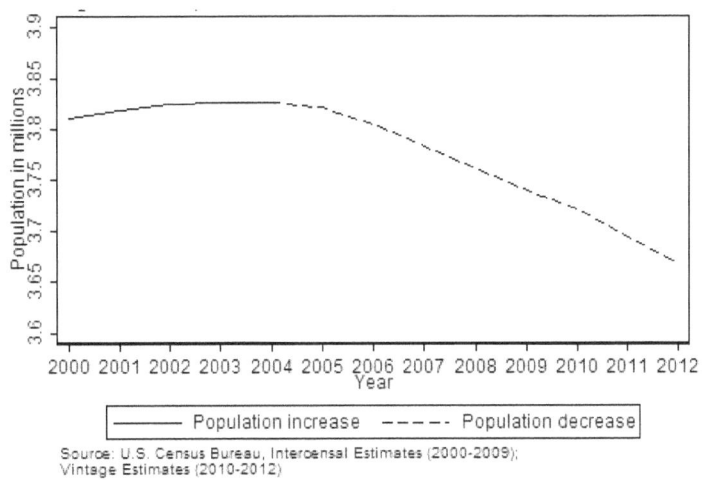

Source: U.S. Census Bureau, Intercensal Estimates (2000-2009);
Vintage Estimates (2010-2012)

Besides age, the education level characterizes the emigrants from the rest of the population in Puerto Rico. Until 2010, Puerto Ricans who abandoned the island had a tendency to be more academically prepared than those who stayed on the island. That was indicated by the percentage of emigrants with college studies. For that reason, some people categorized the most recent exodus of Puerto Ricans to the United States as a "brain drain." That term has been debated for a long time; however, the reality is that the island cannot afford to continue losing their best young talent due to emigration. Figure 4 compares the percentage of emigrants and immigrants with at least some post-secondary education in the past years (Figure 4).

The country getting the most from the mass emigration is the United States. The United States is receiving some of the best talent the island has to offer. The United States is recruiting young workers from the rest of the world, and Puerto Rico is not an exception. The government of Puerto Rico needs to be aware about the implication of the exodus, especially to the economy. Emigration is accelerating the aging of the population and reducing the workforce. According to the Puerto Rico Department of Labor and Human Resources, the total labor force and the number of workers decreased considerably during the last seven years. Since July 2006 to July 2013, the labor force participation rate decreased 17.1%, and the number of employees declined 19.5%.[4] These are troublesome numbers for an economy with seven years of recession. With the constant emigration and the aging of the population, these numbers will continue to decline. The government will have to make the necessary adjustments and face this reality.

Figure 4. Percent of migrants with any post-secondary education or more

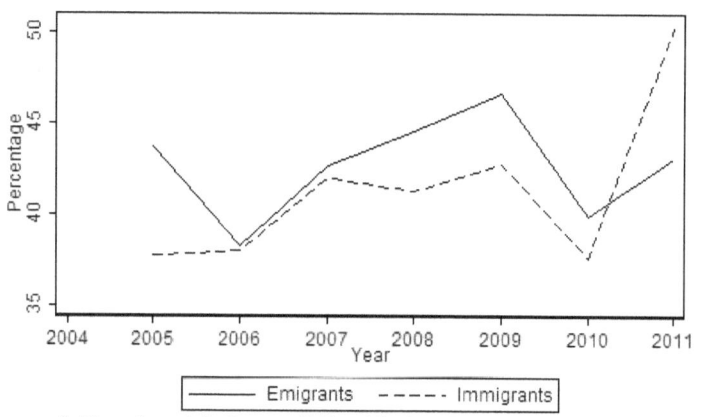

Rodriguez-Ayuso, I. R.; Geerman, K; Marazi-Santiago, M. (2012). Perfil del Migrante, 2011. San Juan, Puerto Rico. Obtenido de www.estadisticas.gobierno.pr.

---

[4] Puerto Rico Department of Labor and Human Resources. Annual Series of Employment and Unemployment in Puerto Rico, July 2013. Retrieved from http://www.trabajo.pr.gov

The demographic changes have been a determining factor to the current recession, which began a few years after the population started to decline. Mario Marazzi, director of the Puerto Rico Institute of Statistics, indicated that at least 25% of the recession was caused by the decrease in population. He stated that, as the population shrinks, the economy is automatically reduced since the economy depends on the patterns of consumption of the human beings.[5] This is worrisome news because there is no evidence that either emigration or the loss of the population will diminish anytime soon. With fewer people on the island, the government could struggle to retain a taxpayer's contribution base that is productive enough to maintain the economy afloat.

───────────────────────

[5] Vera, I. (2013, May 16). Baja en población reduce la economía local [Decrease in population reduces the local economy]. El Vocero. Retrieved from http://www.vocero.com

Pushing Factors

Most of the time, the people depart to other countries for one or more reasons. We call these reasons the pushing factors. In Puerto Rico, the economy has been and continues to be the main pushing factor. The lack of jobs and the sub-employment is a serious dilemma in the country. The unemployment rate in Puerto Rico has not been under 10% in 13 years.[6] At the same time, the labor force participation rate dropped quickly to 41% in July 2013. The economy lost 2.2% of the formal employees (23,000) between July 2012 and July 2013, when its looks like for every job created, there were two or three lost. At the same time, the overall workforce (which includes the people working or looking for work), got smaller by 2.8% or 34,000 workers.

Recent job creation efforts have not been providing the expected results. Data for the first seven months of 2013 from the Puerto Rico Department of Labor and Human Resources[7] suggested that the number of lost jobs surpassed the number of jobs created, resulting in a negative net balance. The effect of this to the economy has been more people who are unemployed, discouraged, or not in the labor force. Another issue regarding the most recent jobs created or announced was that most of

---

[6] Puerto Rico Department of Labor and Human Resources. Annual Series of Employment and Unemployment in Puerto Rico, July 2013. Retrieved from http://www.trabajo.pr.gov
[7] This is the same data reported in the U.S. Bureau of Labor Statistics (BLS).

them were for fast-food and department stores.[8] These jobs might be appropriate for part of the population, but not good enough for the educated youth workforce that has been abandoning the country. The majority of the time, the youth professional workforce, cannot find appropriate job alternatives in Puerto Rico. The lack of specialized jobs for high-skilled people, and the wage difference between Puerto Rico and the United States have been key reasons for the exodus. Each year, many young professionals in their more productive ages are seduced by better job opportunities and higher incomes in the United States and other countries.

Figure 5. Labor force and employment, Puerto Rico
January 2003 to July 2013

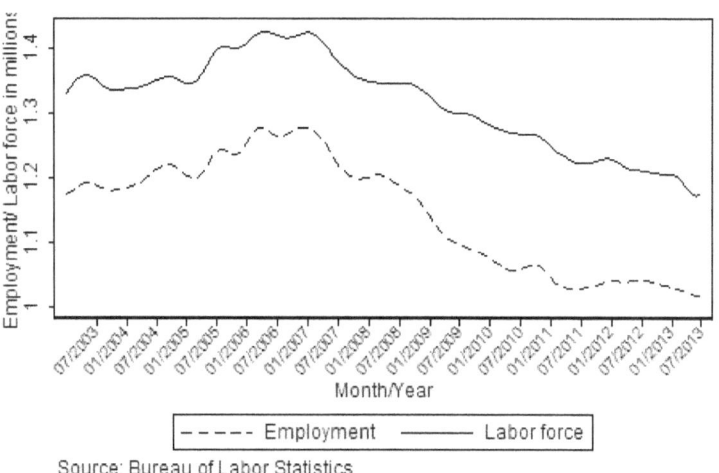

Source: Bureau of Labor Statistics

---

[8] Gómez, A. R. (2013, January 13). Compromisos de sobre 10,000 nuevos empleos en cumbre de Fomento [Commitments of over 10,000 new jobs in Fomento summit]. El Nuevo Día. Retrieved from http://www.elnuevodia.com

If there is one certain thing in Puerto Rico, it is the grim economic situation. According to the U.S. Census Bureau, during 2012, the proportion of people in Puerto Rico living under the poverty level was the highest among the United States jurisdictions.[9] The percentage of people under the poverty levels (44.9%) was much higher than in Mississippi, the state with the highest poverty level in the nation (24.2%). While thousands of people were losing their homes and filling bankruptcies each year, the cost of some of the most essential products and utilities increased. Water, milk, bread and fuel were among the products where costs escalated during the first months of 2013. At the same time, the government added taxes that sum over $1.4 billion.[10]

The new taxes were the result of the government of Puerto Rico been on the brink of bankruptcy and desperate to find solutions to the fiscal problems. The current administration claimed that all the new taxes were indispensable to protect the country's credit, but many economists believed these decisions will sink the economy even further.[11] It is necessary to point out that what is good for the fiscal situation of the government might not necessary be good for the people. Even if the taxes save the credit of the colony, it does not mean that Puerto Rico will

---

[9] United States Census Bureau / American FactFinder. "GCT1701: Percent of People Below Poverty Level in the Past 12 Months (For Whom Poverty Status is Determined)." 2012 American Community Survey. U.S. Census Bureau's American Community Survey Office, 2012. Retrieved from http://factfinder2.census.gov

[10] Rivera, I. (2013, May 1). García Padilla justifica nuevos impuestos para cuadrar presupuesto [García Padilla justifies new taxes to balance budget]. El Nuevo Día. Retrieved from http://www.elnuevodia.com

[11] Álvarez, A. (2013, September 4). Empeorará la crisis económica [The economic crisis will get worse]. El Vocero. Retrieved from http://www.vocero.com

have a healthy economy. Increasing taxes to reach a defined level of revenue or to please some particular groups could create a vicious cycle, which could discourage work and promote further emigration.

Table 1. Top ten jurisdictions by poverty level, 2012

State	Poverty
Puerto Rico	44.9
Mississippi	24.2
New Mexico	20.8
Louisiana	19.9
Arkansas	19.8
Kentucky	19.4
Georgia	19.2
Alabama	19.0
Arizona	18.7
South Carolina	18.3

Source: U.S. Census Bureau, American Community Survey 2012

Most of the data suggests that the economy is still deteriorating. In addition to the employment issues, the Government Development Bank Economic Activity Index (GDB-EAI) had a year over year decrease of 5% by July 2013.[12] The GDB-EAI is considered a coincident index[13] for the economic activity in Puerto Rico, which is highly correlated with the level and annual growth of the real Gross National Product (GNP). If this

---

[12] Puerto Rico Government Development Bank. (2013). Economic Indicators - Time Series. Retrieved October 4, 2013, from http://www.gdbpr.com
[13] The coincident indexes combine four indicators to summarize current economic conditions in a single statistic. The four indicators in the coincident index are: (a) the total non-farm payroll employment, (b) cement sales, (c) gasoline consumption, and (d) electric power generation.

index is decreasing, the annual growth of the real GNP will certainly follow a similar trend.

**Figure 6. Puerto Rico Economic Activity Index,
July 2004 to July 2013**

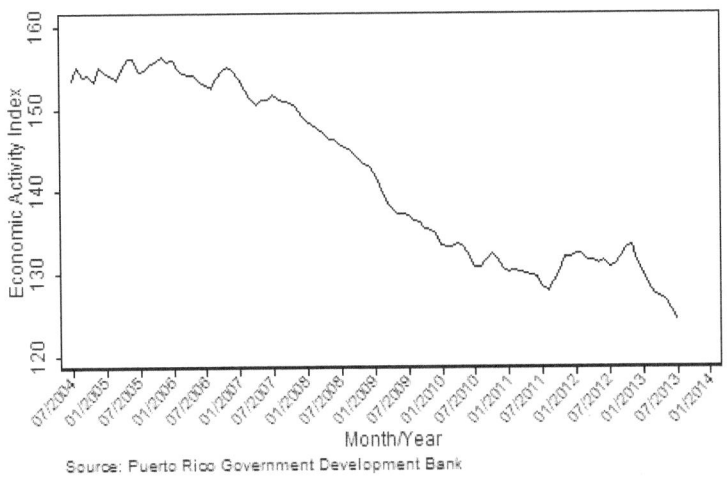

Source: Puerto Rico Government Development Bank

The economic situation combined with the precarious fiscal situation of the country will continue to be the central pushing factor for the residents of Puerto Rico. The government is focusing on resolving the fiscal problems, including a public debt of $70 billion that reached 96% of the GNP[14] and the credit rating agencies threatening to downgrade the credit of Puerto Rico to junk status. Such a negative perspective could promote that more people abandon Puerto Rico in the near future. The uncertainty with the economic situation of Puerto Rico is so immense

---

[14] Pelatti, L. G. (2013). La deuda pública marca un nuevo récord y ya alcanza el 96% del PNB [The public debt marks a new record, and has already reached 96% of the GNP]. Sin Comillas. Retrieved August 19, from http://sincomillas.com

that, if left unresolved, will create such a poor prospect that might push aside potential business and workers.

Improving the economic situation might not be enough to slow or reverse the current migration flow to the United States. There are other elements that are considered by the people leaving the country. One significant factor is violence, which has reached epidemic proportions in Puerto Rico. There is no doubt that Puerto Rico is a violent country. The crime rates have skyrocketed as well as other violence indicators. Interpersonal violence has permeated the homes, the schools, the workplaces, and the streets of Puerto Rico. Violence is commonplace in Puerto Ricans daily lives. It is so frequent that people have adapted to live with it. The lack of respect for the life of others is evident, and it takes a bizarre act of violence to cause consternation and disapproval from the people in Puerto Rico. People often respond to violence with more violence, and the opposition of the current government expects high crime rates in order to use that as a campaign slogan.

The most severe level of violence is the act of murder. The number of deaths by murders in Puerto Rico exceeds those of any recent epidemic, but it has not been considered as such. In 2011, the murder rate in Puerto Rico was the highest among the United States jurisdictions.[15] The island was also ranked among the top 20 most homicidal countries in the world.[16] The number of murders and non-negligent manslaughter in

[15] Refers to the 50 states, Washington D.C. and Puerto Rico.
[16] Goldschein, E. (2011, December 1). The 20 Most Homicidal Countries in the World. Business Insider. Retrieved from http://www.businessinsider.com

Puerto Rico (1,136) in 2011 was only exceeded by California (1,792), a state with 10 times the number of residents of Puerto Rico.[17] In 2012, only California, Florida and Texas surpassed Puerto Rico in the numbers of murders; however, because of the total population, the colony continued to have the highest murder rate among all the jurisdictions. Washington D.C. had the second highest rate with 13.9 murders per 100,000 inhabitants, compared to 26.7 murders per 100,000 inhabitants in Puerto Rico.[18]

Table 2. Top ten jurisdictions by murder rate, 2012

Jurisdiction	Murder rate
Puerto Rico	26.7
District of Columbia	13.9
Louisiana	10.8
Mississippi	7.4
Alabama	7.1
Michigan	7.0
South Carolina	6.9
Missouri	6.5
Maryland	6.3
Delaware	6.2

Rate by 100,000 inhabitants
Source: Federal Bureau of Investigation, Uniform Crime Report 2012

---

[17] Federal Bureau of Investigation, Uniform Crime Report 2011. Retrieved from http://www.fbi.gov
[18] Federal Bureau of Investigation, Uniform Crime Report 2012. Retrieved from http://www.fbi.gov

Even Vieques, a small municipality with just 9,300 inhabitants, and one of the main tourist attractions in Puerto Rico has been marked by violence. The municipality was in the middle of a violent war that resulted in 15 murders during the first 10 months of the year 2013.[19] The latter means that the number of murders in Vieques exceeds the total number of murders in the states of Vermont and Wyoming during 2012, and was equal to the number of murders in New Hampshire for the same year.

The homicides[20] in Puerto Rico were so high in 2011 that they ranked as the sixth leading cause of death in the country and the fourth cause of death among the males. The age group most affected by the homicides was young males (15-29 years of age) with 54% of the deaths. Homicides were the main cause of death for all the five-year age groups from 15 to 39 years of ages.

The government needs to treat the violence crisis as a public health problem. The current approach, which focuses on the criminal justice system, has proven to be ineffective. Even with the jails approaching the maximum capacity, with 34 inmates per 10,000 inhabitants[21] and with over 1.8 million criminal cases attended by the judicial system during the

---

[19] Alvarado, G. E. (2013, October 30). Azotada por la delincuencia [Plagued by the crime]. El Nuevo Día. Retrieved from http://www.elnuevodia.com

[20] The Vital Statistics System use the term homicides instead of murders in the classification of cause of deaths. A study by the Puerto Rico Institute of Statistics called Report to the Board of Directors on the Comparability of Statistics on Murders and Homicides established the difference between the two terms.

[21] Puerto Rico Department of Corrections and Rehabilitation, Correctional Population Report of Daily Average (Monthly/Annual) for July 2013.

last decade,[22] violence does not seem to decrease. It is time to recognize that a public health approach is essential to prevent and reduce the violence in Puerto Rico. This approach has various steps: (a) define and monitor the problem, (b) identify risk and protective factors, (c) develop and test prevention strategies, and (d) ensure widespread adoption.[23] The recently published Profile of Violence in Puerto Rico: 1984 - 2004 is an example of the work related to the first steps in the public health approach to violence prevention. That publication identified the dimensions and causes of violence in Puerto Rico.

Other literature identified some of the most common risk factors associated with violence and some prevention strategies that could work in Puerto Rico. These studies need to be analyzed, and efforts need to be made to develop evidence-based prevention strategies that are culturally competent for Puerto Rico. The government alone cannot deal with this public health issue. Coalitions could be built to help in all steps of the public health approach to violence prevention. The government also needs to invest more resources in order to prevent violence. A formal prevention program needs to be established, and more resources should be assigned to prevention efforts. The toll of violence is too big to postpone the implementation of the necessary changes that could help alleviate this burden in the future.

---

[22] Bauzá, N. (2013, October 3). Rama Judicial atendió casi dos millones de casos en la última década [Judicial Branch deal with nearly two million cases in the last decade]. El Nuevo Día. Retrieved from http://www.elnuevodia.com

[23] Centers for Disease Control and Prevention, National Center for Injury Prevention and Control, & Division of Violence Prevention. (2011). The Public Health Approach to Violence Prevention. http://www.cdc.gov

People are aware of the violence that permeates in Puerto Rico, and this situation is influencing their decision to leave the country. They also noticed the level of corruption within the agencies and organizations responsible for ensuring the safety of the population. Corruption taints the police and the legal system in the country. The federal government made one of the largest raids of police corruption in Puerto Rico. During that raid, federal agents arrested over 90 local police officers who were involved in drug dealing and other criminal activities. The federal government also made an agreement with the local police to overcome a long history of discrimination, violence and corruption in the Puerto Rico Police Department.[24] The judicial system also has its share of problems. The Federal Bureau of Investigation (FBI) has been aware of the behavior of the judicial system in Puerto Rico and formed a working group dedicated to investigate the system.[25] The federal government also took over high profile cases that were mishandled by local authorities.

The education and health systems are relevant pushing factors for some of the emigrants. The public education system continually fails to be prepared for the beginning of the academic year. Each year, the same problems, where there are school facilities in bad conditions and lack of teachers for essential courses, resurface. Meanwhile, according to the School Profile for Puerto Rico prepared by the Puerto Rico Department

---

[24] Álvarez, L. (2013, July 17). Agreement Is Reached on Police Reforms in Puerto Rico, The New York Times. Retrieved from http://www.nytimes.com

[25] Rivera, M. E. (2013, August 27). FBI creará escuadrón especializado en corrupción judicial. [FBI will create squad specialized in judicial corruption]. Noticel. Retrieved from http://www.noticel.com

of Education, 87% of the schools were under heavy scrutiny because of low levels of academic achievement by the students during the academic year of 2011-2012. This means that the majority of the schools were on an improvement plan, established by Puerto Rico Department of Education, in order to improve the academic performance.

Considering the aforementioned data, it seems that the Department of Education failed to deliver quality education, despite spending a quarter of the consolidated budget from the general fund. The Department of Education budget for the fiscal year 2013-2014 was 53% higher than for the fiscal year 2000-2001,[26] but there were 32% fewer students in the system.[27] In the past year, the budget increased despite a decrease in students' enrollment. An ineffective education system is a critical pushing factor for young parents looking for a better education for their children.

Regarding the health system, one of the main issues has been the lack or limited availability of health professionals. This issue has resulted, in part, by the exodus of physicians and other health professionals. The number of physicians has diminished by 12.7% since 2008;[28] some specialties are so scarce that scheduling an appointment is burdensome. Some geographic areas within the island are also devoid of certain

---

[26] Commonwealth of Puerto Rico, Budgets information retrieved from http://www.presupuesto.pr.gov

[27] U.S. Department of Education, National Center for Education Statistics, Common Core of Data. Obtained via email from the Puerto Rico Institute of Statistics.

[28] Puerto Rico está sufriendo un éxodo de médicos [Puerto Rico is suffering an exodus of doctors]. (2013, April 18). Fox News Latino. Retrieved from http://latino.foxnews.com

medical specialties. The lack of physicians with certain medical specialties has forced some people to seek medical treatment in the United States. This situation is unfavorable for Puerto Rico because the states continue recruiting health professionals from the island. If the trend continues, in the near future, Puerto Rico might not be able to afford the impending increase in the demand for health services caused by the aging of the population.

Other pushing factors contributing to the exodus of Puerto Ricans include the political instability of the island and the cost of living. The lack of pulling factors decreases the chances of return migration or immigration of people from other countries. Immigration is necessary to prevent a further decline in the population. If the government of Puerto Rico expects to stop or reverse the loss of the population, the core pushing factors need to be addressed. Of great importance will be the creation of professional and competitive jobs for people younger than 34 years of age, who make up the bulk of emigrants. This group will continue to abandon the country if their unemployment rate of 21.1% of July 2013 persists.[29] For them, there are few reasons to stay and a lot of reasons to leave.

In summary, as a result of their political status, Puerto Ricans have a unique opportunity to migrate to another country, which they perceive have better job opportunities, quality of life, education and health systems, and less violence. The pushing factors out-weight the pulling

---

[29] Puerto Rico Department of Labor and Human Resource, Working Group Survey, July 2013. Retrieved from http://www.trabajo.pr.gov

factors, and Puerto Ricans see the United States as a valve of escape from the island. Therefore, most Puerto Ricans buy a one-way ticket, without considering a comeback.

Replacement Shortage

Migration is not the only demographic component contributing to the reduction of the population. The decline in births has been a decisive factor in the occurrence of this demographic phenomenon. Women in Puerto Rico are not having the number of children necessary to counteract emigration. The total fertility rate for 2010 was 1.6 children per woman.[30] This rate was below the 2.1 children per woman required to achieve the population replacement level. Preliminary data for 2011 indicated that the fertility continued to decline even further. In the future, if the current fertility rates remain stable or decrease, live births will not be sufficient to produce a natural increase Puerto Rico's population.

The demographic components of migration, birth and death are closely related, and changes in one component affect the others. In that sense, the mass exodus of young people has been a determining factor in the reduction of live births in Puerto Rico. The number of live births in Puerto Rico was reduced by 29%, from 59,460 live births in 2000 to 42,203 in 2010.[31] During that period, the number of live births to women of Puerto Rican origin increased by 14.2% in the United State from

---

[30] Puerto Rico Department of Health (2012). 2009 and 2010 Vital Statistics Report: Births, Marriages and Divorces.
[31] Puerto Rico Department of Health, Statistical Analysis Division.

58,124 live births in 2000 to 66,368 in 2010.[32] Even the number of live births by women of Puerto Rican origin younger than 30 years in the United States (47,810) exceeded the number of live births in Puerto Rico during 2010. Many of these live births were from women who migrated to the United States during the last decade. Instead of having children in Puerto Rico these women had them in the United States.

The decline in live births has been reported in all the maternal age groups. The age-specific fertility rate for teenage mothers was reduced by 28% between 2000 and 2010. In the other age groups, the total fertility rate declined between 12.4% and 22.2% (Figure 7). Women in Puerto Rico are not only having fewer children, but also postponing having them until an older age. In 1990, 8.7% of women having their first child had at least 30 years of age; that percentage increased to 14.7% in 2010. The longer women wait to have children, fewer children will be born. Additionally, having future generations with fewer women in childbearing ages will result in fewer births.

---

[32] Centers for Disease Control and Prevention, National Center for Health Statistics, National Vital Statistics Report (2002) Vol.50 Number 5 and National Vital Statistics Report (2012) Vol.61 Number 1.

**Figure 7. Percent change of age-specific fertility rates,
Puerto Rico 2000-2010**

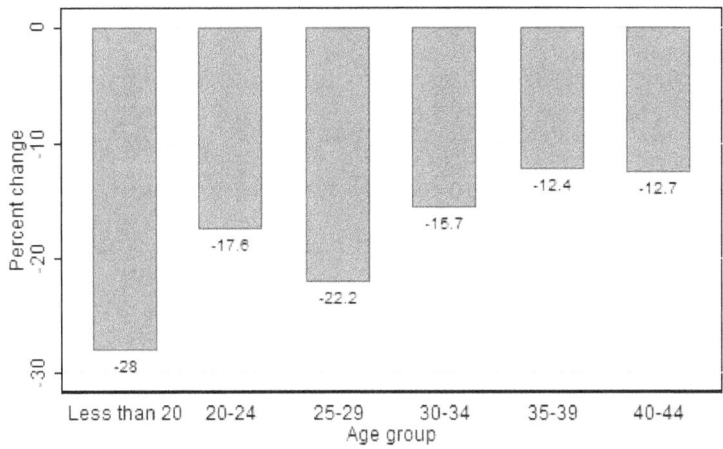

Source: Puerto Rico Department of Health, Statistical Analysis Division

There are several factors determining why women have fewer children and conceive them at older ages. Some of these factors relate to the
fact that more women are completing higher education levels and are
more active in the formal economy of the country. While women have
been taking their rightful place in the economy, they are making the
decision to postpone the moment of having children or not having them at
all. Generally, the business environment and the employers do not
facilitate that women who want to have children continue to have their
job responsibilities or even achieve higher positions. It is necessary to
make adjustments that facilitate the life of working mothers and allow
them to have the number of children they wish, without having to worry
about the consequences of their decision in their employment status.
Each year more women are responsible breadwinners for their families,
and more people depend on their careers. These women also confront a

more competitive business environment. For these women, staying at home to raise their children might not be an option even if they want it.

The economic situation, especially the high rate of unemployment, is another factor that discourages having children. Given the current economic circumstances, the young people who have not migrated avoid having children. This is also one of the reasons many couples are post-poning marriage until they are more economically prepared. During 2012, there were more women of 15 years of age or more never married compared to a few decades ago. For example, in 2000, 25% of the women of 15 years of age or more were never married. That percentage reached 35% in 2012. For that year, 64.5% of the women 20 to 34 years of age and 28.2% of the women 35 to 44 years of age were never married.[33] In addition to the drop in live births, this caused a proliferation in the percentage of live births outside marriage.

The interaction between the demographic components will reach a level in which eventually the population will stop its natural growth. This means that there will be more deaths than live births. To obtain the natural growth, a person needs to subtract the number of deaths to the number of live births. As long as the number of live births exceeds the number of deaths, the natural growth will be positive, and the population will grow naturally. A community with these characteristics will contin-ue to see an increase in the total population as long as the migration

---

[33] United States Census Bureau / American FactFinder. "S1201: Marital Status". 2012 American Community Survey. U.S. Census Bureau's American Community Survey Office, 2012. Retrieved from http://factfinder2.census.gov

allows it. In Puerto Rico's case, the number of people who leave the country is so significant that the natural growth is not enough to maintain an increase in the population. That is why the population is shrinking even when there are more births than deaths.

Figure 8. Natural growth, Puerto Rico 2000 to 2010

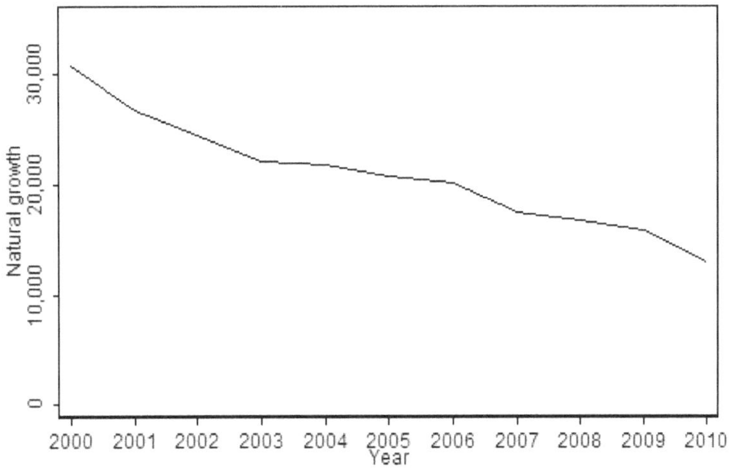

Source: Puerto Rico Department of Health, Statistical Analysis Division

In 2011, some of the municipalities (county equivalent) in Puerto Rico had a larger number of deaths than births; therefore, these munici-palities were losing population in a natural way. During 2011, in the municipality of Mayagüez 881 people died while 848 infants were born.[34] A similar pattern is presented in the municipality of Hormigueros in the same year. Eventually, this will be a widespread phenomenon in Puerto Rico. This has been the experience in other countries like Russia, Italy,

---

[34] Puerto Rico Department of Health, Statistical Analysis Division.

Hungary, and Japan[35] that like Puerto Rico have an extremely old age structure.

The number of deaths has experienced minimal changes over the past few years, but the aging of the population could alter that trend. With more people in older age groups, the number of deaths could rise, mainly because elders have a higher risk of dying than young people. This does not necessary means that the risk of dying in Puerto Rico will be higher, but that there will be more people (elders) with higher risk of mortality.

The main change in mortality has been in the relative importance of the causes of death. Preliminary data from the Puerto Rico Department of Health suggest that, during 2011, cancer became the first cause of death in Puerto Rico. The latter occurred mainly because of a large decrease in deaths by heart diseases, which was the main cause of death in the previous decades. Diabetes continues to be the third leading cause of death.

According to the 2010 mortality data for Puerto Rico, diabetes was the only cause within the first three causes of death with an increasing risk of dying of that cause. The cause with the biggest increase in term of the number and risk of death has been Alzheimer Disease. This cause of death ranked fourth in 2010 among the leading causes of deaths. This position is five spots higher than in 2000, when this condition was the ninth cause of death. The age-adjusted mortality rate for this cause increased by 94.5% from the year 2000 to the year 2010 (Table 3).

---

[35] CIA World Factbook Country Comparison: Birth Rate and CIA World Factbook Country Comparison: Death Rate. Retrieved from https://www.cia.gov

Table 3. Top ten causes of death in Puerto Rico, 2010

Cause	Num.	Age-adjusted rate 2010	Age-adjusted rate 2000
Hearth diseases	5,208	125.7	189.2
Malignant neoplasms (cancer)	5,197	123.8	138.9
Diabetes mellitus	2,959	70.4	69.7
Alzheimer's disease	1,863	46.1	23.7
Cerebrovascular diseases	1,507	36.7	49.9
Chronic lower respiratory diseases	1,092	26.5	35.9
Accidents	1,028	26.2	40.3
Nephritis, nephrotic syndrome and nephrosis	989	23.8	23.0
Homicides	967	26.3	17.6
Pneumonia and influenza	821	20.0	30.9

Source: Puerto Rico Department of Health, Statistical Analysis Division

All the conditions mentioned above are more common in older people than in younger ones. These chronic diseases are the leading causes of death in Puerto Rico. However, as stated previously, during the past decade, homicides were frequently positioned in the top 10 spots among all causes of deaths. Generally, this cause of death is more prevalent among young people. Death by this cause increases the years of life lost, which influence the life expectancy of the population.

The decline in the population is a phenomenon that few countries in the world have experienced, and Puerto Rico was the first in the Americas to present this new demographic reality. If no changes occur, the trends of migration, birth, and death rates suggest that the population of Puerto Rico will continue to decline for several years. Therefore, at some point Puerto Rico could have more people dying than babies crying at birth.

Inverted Pyramid

Puerto Rico is undergoing a deep transformation induced by remarkable demographic changes. The age structure of the population of Puerto Rico is changing; specifically, it is getting older at a fast pace. The aging of the population is a global phenomenon and one of public health greatest achievement. Despite this, by extending the life of the people, countries could encounter new challenges not found in younger populations.

While developing countries have a tendency of having younger populations, developed countries are already facing the challenges of older age structures. Countries like Japan, Italy, Greece, Spain, and Germany have a median age over 40, meaning that half of their people are at least 40 years of age or older.[36] For most of these countries, the aging of their population has been a slow process, spanning many years, but for the developing countries, the process will be much faster. For example, it took France 115 years to duplicate the percentage of people with 65 years of age or more from 7% to 14%; on the other hand, it is estimated that it will take Brazil less than 25 years for the same phenomenon to occur.[37] It took Puerto Rico less than 40 year for that process to occur.

---

[36] CIA World Factbook Country Comparison: Median Age. Retrieved from https://www.cia.gov

[37] Huenchuan, S. (2013). Ageing, solidarity and social protection in Latin America and the Caribbean: Economic Commission for Latin America and the Caribbean (ECLAC). Retrieved from www.eclac.org

Generally, the aging of the population is the result of increasing life expectancy and declining birth rates. The life expectancy in Puerto Rico went from a low life expectancy of 40.6 years of age in 1930, to a high life expectancy of over 60 years of age in 1950. The life expectancy at birth of 79 years of age in 2009 was comparable to developed countries like Portugal, Denmark, and the United States.[38] Women have a higher life expectancy than men. In 2009, the difference in life expectancy between women and men was almost 8 years.[39]

As mentioned in the previous chapter, the fertility rate in Puerto Rico is also falling. The fertility in Puerto Rico is 1.6 children per women, and the numbers of live births are at the lowest levels in the history of the vital record system. In summary, the population is aging because people are living longer while having fewer children.

Puerto Rico has a third significant factor associated with the aging of the population. The Puerto Rico Institute of Statistics confirmed that the majority of the emigrants between 2000 and 2010 were people with younger ages, compared to the ones who remained on the island. This means that the recent exodus of Puerto Ricans has sped up the aging of the population. Emigration has lowered the number and percentage of young people on the island since they represented the bulk of migrants. Thousands of young men and women in reproductive ages abandoned the country each year, which affected the fertility rates and the age distribu-

---

[38] CIA World Factbook Country Comparison: Life Expectancy at Birth. Retrieved from https://www.cia.gov
[39] Puerto Rico Department of Health (2013). Abridged life tables for Puerto Rico: 1999-2001 to 2008-2010.

tion of the island. If these people had opted for staying in Puerto Rico, they would have had their children in the island instead of in the United States, or the other countries of destination. Therefore, the future generation is considerably reduced by emigration.

While the overall population of Puerto Rico is decreasing, the number of elders is rising. The population of 65 years of age or more grew by 27.5% between 2000 and 2010, and for the first time, this group exceeded the number of youngsters who are less than 10 years old. The age structure, that was considered old in the year 2000, reached in 2010 a level comparable to the developed countries in the world. The median age reached 36 years in 2010, and the percentage of people 65 years old or more wind up to 14.5% of the population (Figure 9). Since women live longer than men, they also had an older age structure, with a median age of 38.6 years in 2010 compared to a median of 35.1 years for men.[40] Females represented 56.4% of the population of 65 years of age or more in 2010. That year, all the municipalities, had a median age of over 30 years, which was considered old.

---

[40] United States Census Bureau / American FactFinder. "DP-1: Profile of General Population and Housing Characteristics: 2010". 2010 Census. U.S. Census Bureau, 2010. Retrieved from http://factfinder2.census.gov

**Figure 9. Percent of population 65 years of age or more,
Puerto Rico, 1950 to 2010**

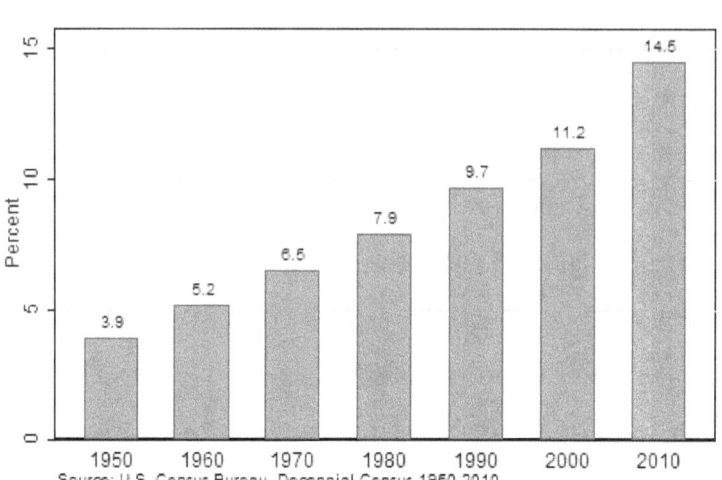

Source: U.S. Census Bureau, Decennial Census 1950-2010

The aging of the population is a process that will continue. The proportion of people with 65 years or more in Puerto Rico is projected to reach 32.2% of the population by the year 2050.[41] This would make Puerto Rico one of the older countries worldwide. Projections show that Puerto Rico will have an upside-down (inverted) population pyramid, with the majority of the people in older age groups (Figure 10).

---

[41] U.S. Census Bureau, International Database. Retrieved from
http://www.census.gov

Figure 10. Population pyramids, Puerto Rico 2010 and 2050

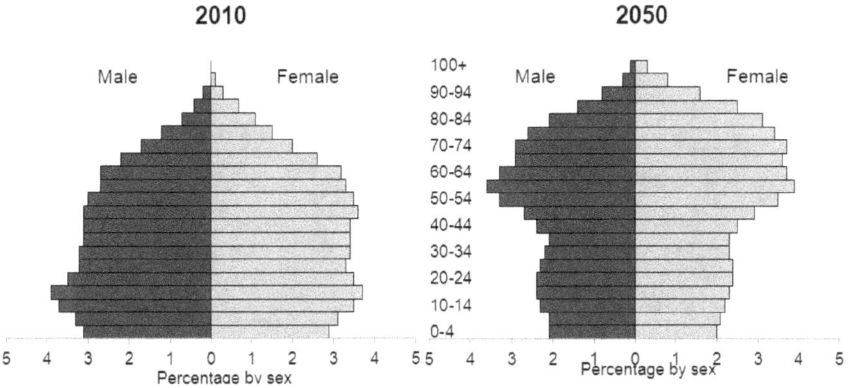

Source U.S. Census Bureau, International Database

The projections have the population of Puerto Rico dropping to just 2.3 million people by the year 2050. This is comparable to the population that Puerto Rico had in 1960. However, the age structure will differ since, in 2050, people 65 years of age or more will outnumber the population under 35 years of age, and the majority of the people will have 50 years of age or more. Puerto Rico will have more elders even when it is expected that the country will have 1.5 million fewer persons compared to the population of 2010. The projections also present a scenario where the number of elder women will surpass the number of women in reproductive ages (15 to 44 years of ages) in 2039. By 2050, the number of women in reproductive age will have decreased 57% compared to 2010 (Table 4).

**Table 4. Expected female population change by age,
Puerto Rico 2010 and 2050**

Age	2010	2050	Percent change
Less than 15	355,421	147,898	-58.4%
15 to 44	774,245	334,168	-56.8%
45 to 64	501,101	328,814	-34.4%
65 or more	308,239	448,182	45.4%

Source: U.S. Census Bureau, International Database.

A shrinking population, that at the same time is getting older, presents a challenge to the government of Puerto Rico. The current and future administrations need to make a plan to deal with all the possible situations these demographic changes could cause. Not being prepared for the aging of the population could have an effect on the economy and the ability to provide resources and services for this population. The government needs to establish a long-term strategy to deal with the imminent demographic challenges of an elder community before it is too late.

Challenges and Implications

Puerto Rico is facing numerous challenges caused, in part, by the aging of the population. These challenges range from fewer people in working ages, a collapse of the housing market, an increase in the demand of health services, and an insolvent public retirement system, among others. Most of these challenges have been overlooked for decades. Furthermore, these issues were disregarded by each administration that passed the pressure of resolving the issues to the next administration. Eventually, some of these challenges reached a point in which the consequence of continuing to ignore them could be catastrophic.

The window of opportunities is closing fast, and actions are required to safe Puerto Rico from a catastrophe. The government failed to acknowledge the effects of the demographic changes for too long, and now, the economy is suffering the consequences. The economy is sinking and the government is trying to keep it afloat, but the demographic storm is strong. Current and future administrations will need to develop new policies and approaches, which consider the demographic changes, especially the aging of the population.

The aging of the population affects many aspects of Puerto Rico's economy. Puerto Rico lacks the economic growth that characterized the experience of aging in most of the developed countries. In contrast to most of those countries, the colony is getting poorer at the same time as it is getting older. The economic situation does not seem to be improving soon. Official projections predict that the colony's economy will shrink by 0.8 percent during the fiscal year 2014.[42] This is expected since the working population is shrinking at the same time that the older population is increasing. The effect is fewer people contributing to the economic growth and the social support systems.

It is also worrisome the continuous shrinking ratio of people in the most productive working ages, compared to the old population. In the year 2010, there were 4.1 persons of 15 to 64 years of age for every person of 65 years of age or more. This ratio was lower than the ratio in 2000 (5.8). If this trend continues, this ratio will reach a detrimental level in the future after most of the "baby boomers" retire. It is projected that, by the year 2050, the ratio will be 1.7 persons of 15 to 64 years of age for every person of at least 65 years of age. For that reason, it will be indispensable an increase in the labor force participation and production. The economy of Puerto Rico will not survive with a labor force participation rate of just 41% of the population over 15 years of age.[43]

For a colony that wants to be considered at the same level as a developed country, there are too many people outside the labor force. The biggest challenge to increase productivity will be encouraging people to work after decades of promoting poverty and dependence. Historically, it has been easier for government administrations to maintain people in poverty, by receiving federal and local benefits, than aiding them to get

---

[42] Kaske, M. (2013, November 1). Puerto Rico Economy Forecast to Shrink 0.8% in Fiscal 2014, Bloomberg. Retrieved from http://www.bloomberg.com

[43] Puerto Rico Department of Labor and Human Resource, Working Group Survey, July 2013. Retrieved from http://www.trabajo.pr.gov

out of poverty. The end-result is that the number of households receiving food stamp benefits reached a record high of 38% in 2012.[44]

Using the population projections and if Puerto Rico maintains the labor force participation rates by age of July 2013, we can project that fewer than 660,000 people will be part of the labor force during the year 2050. That means that Puerto Rico could lose at least 44% of the total workforce by that year if the participation rates do not rise. Since the labor force participation and the number of workers are key determinants of the country's economy, their constant decline will continue to affect the economic growth, and be detrimental to the economy.

The demographic transformation will require some urgent decisions regarding the remaining public retirement systems. Without changes, the retirement systems will not overcome the aging of the population. These systems were not designed with the new demographic reality in mind. The systems never evolved in the right direction either. The people who planned these systems did not account for a society with fewer workers and so many people with a longer life expectancy and living off the retirement funds. With the demographic changes, the retirement funds will need to provide money for more people and for a longer time. The current systems are incapable of performing in such way. The retirement systems lack the funds to continue paying for the benefits to retirees without a reform.

---

[44] United States Census Bureau / American FactFinder. "CP03: Selected Economic Characteristics". 2012 American Community Survey. U.S. Census Bureau's American Community Survey Office, 2012. Retrieved from http://factfinder2.census.gov

Recently, the retirement system of the general government had a reform that occurred too late. This resulted in severe consequence to the workers. With that reform, the government decided that current and future generations of public workers will pay the price for the delay in the retirement system reform. As part of the reform, the age of retirement was increased, the workers' contribution was raised, and benefits for future retirees were reduced or eliminated.

Next in line for a reform is the teachers' retirement system. Reforming this system will have an additional difficulty since teachers do not contribute to the Social Security system. This means that retirement funds could be their only source of income after retirement. It is expected that the government will implement changes similar to the ones mentioned before to this retirement system, and many people will suffer the consequences. These situations should serve as an example to the government regarding the effect of delaying changes instead of working on them when they are required.

Maintaining a healthy population is going to be another challenge with the increase of the elder population. Older people get sick more often and have higher prevalence rates of chronic diseases than the younger people. The prevalence of chronic diseases in adults and especially the elder population is high in Puerto Rico. The prevalence of diabetes for the adult population was 16.4%, the highest among the United States jurisdictions in the year 2012.[45] Meanwhile, one of every

---

[45] Centers for Disease Control and Prevention, Behavioral Risk Factor Surveillance System (BRFSS). Retrieved from http://www.cdc.gov/brfss

three people (35%) of 65 years of age or more had diabetes. The high-level of prevalence of other chronic diseases and risk factors like hypertension (36.8% in 2011) and overweight and obesity (66.2% in 2012) is another source of concern. All of these chronic diseases have an upward tendency. The increase in the prevalence of diabetes is noteworthy. From 2000 to 2010, the prevalence of diabetes for the adult population increased 4.2 percent points (8.5% to 12.8%). Although not comparable with past data,[46] diabetes prevalence for 2012 (16.4%) increased when compared to the data of 2011 (13.5%). Diabetes was also one of the few causes of death for with the actual risk of dying has been increasing. The government will have to promote a more active and healthy aging to reduce the prevalence of chronic diseases in the future.

Puerto Rico also has a shortage of specialized physicians and other health professionals to take care of future health needs as a result of an aging population. This is a problem that could get worse with the continuing emigration waves of these professionals leaving to the United States. The expected increase in demand of health services, caused by the aging of the population, will soon expose this deficiency and affect the quality of health services in Puerto Rico.

The health authorities need to look out for alternatives and strategies to overcome the tendency of health professionals that are abandoning Puerto Rico. With an increased elder population, the government needs

---

[46] The Behavioral Risk Factor Surveillance System (BRFSS) experienced a methodology change starting with the 2011 data. Some of the new data is not comparable with the data of previous years.

to establish a goal to make sure the people live healthier, productive, and longer lives. The lack of health professionals could jeopardize this goal and affect other important areas like the economy.

Another challenge will be the long-term care of the elder population. The demand for these services is bound to increase with the aging of the population. Given this scenario, who is going to take care of this population? The elders will need support services like housekeepers, home nursing, residential care, community care, long-stay hospitals, and transportation to health services. With fewer workers in the future, the availability of caregivers could decrease. Also, with continued emigration, the increased number of divorces, more adults without a child, and more children being raised in single-parent households, more people will have minimal or nonexistent family support and care. This will leave the government with a more prominent role in the long-term care of the older population. These situations raise the question of who is going to pay for the long-term care of this group.

Many individuals in Puerto Rico approach older ages with little or no savings. It is estimated that less than half of the households in Puerto Rico have some sort of savings.[47] If this trend continues, the cost of long-term care is going to be a burden, especially for the family. In many occasions, families act as protection mechanisms that absorb part of the economic risks of older people. Currently, there are people with financial and emotional burdens as they support both their children and parents.

---

[47] Toro-Tulla, H. J. (2013). Puerto Rico Survey of Consumer Finances. Center for a New Economy. Retrieved from http://grupocne.org

This could be the norm in the future, and maybe they will have the additional burden of supporting their grandparents.

One challenge that is out-of-control for Puerto Ricans is the colonial status. The main supporting systems in Puerto Rico, in this case Social Security, Medicaid, and Medicare, are controlled by the United States. Puerto Rico does not have a vote for the possible changes in those systems. There is no way Puerto Ricans will know for certain if, at the time of imposing future changes in the systems, the United States will consider the socioeconomic difference between the colony and the states. Therefore, future changes may have a detrimental impact in Puerto Rico.

There are other areas in the society that need to change in order to improve the quality of life of current and future elders. The lack of a reliable collective transportation system is one of the areas of concern. The collective transportation system in Puerto Rico is limited primarily to the metropolitan area surrounding the capital of San Juan. The system is slow and unreliable, with long waiting times and irregular schedules.[48] The demand for collective transportation could increase with the aging of the population. The accessibility and quality of life of Puerto Ricans could be improved with an expansion and reorganization of the collective transportation systems. A better collective transportation system will

---

[48] Villanueva Lugo, J., & Palermo Alvarado, K. M. (2005). Percepión del usuario del transporte colectivo sobre la calidad del servicio ofrecido por la AMA [Collective transportation user's perception of the quality of service offered by the Metropolitan Bus Authority]. Mayagüez: University of Puerto Rico, Mayagüez Campus. Retrieved from http://uprati.uprm.edu/interns/group1_final_reports/jaritcely.pdf

facilitate access to health services, recreational areas, and other relevant places.

Finally, the collapse of the housing market proved that Puerto Rico was not ready for these demographic changes. The number of housing units increased 15.4% between 2000 and 2010.[49] This happened even when the population growth was slow and the population was aging. The construction of new housing units was not on par with the population and economic growth. The aging of the population will continue to be a predicament for housing and the real estate markets. Compared to previous decades, there will be fewer buyers for existing properties. That represents less demand for a constant supply of properties. The fundamental principles of economy dictate that this will lower the prices. The home prices, which dropped up to 35% in some places,[50] might continue to drop if the demand continues the downward trend. According to the American Community Survey, during 2012, the number of vacant properties reached a record high of 20% of the housing units in Puerto Rico.

---

[49] U.S. Census Bureau, Decennial Census 2000 and 2010. Retrieved from http://factfinder2.census.gov
[50] Developers have endured a roller coaster ride. (2010). Caribbean Business. Retrieved from http://www.caribbeanbusinesspr.com

Figure 11. Abandoned house in Puerto Rico

The aging of the population also provides certain benefits and opportunities that are worth mentioning. The latter could provoke a decline in
criminal activities, one of the central pushing factors in Puerto Rico. The
rationale behind this is that the people involved in these criminal activities tend to be younger, and the elders tend to be more law-abiding. If
that indeed happens, that could represent an opportunity to redistribute
some of the resources destined for security to other areas.

The decline of birth represents an opportunity to improve education.
The budget could be used more efficiently by reducing the number of
schools and focusing more on the teaching aspect of the education. In
addition, there could be fewer children per classroom, which benefits
both the students and teachers. The aging of the population also opens up
new business opportunities for people. The market will expand for

caregivers in the health-care sector and for specialized products for the elderly. Puerto Rico have been slow adapting and taking the opportunities that are being provided by this phenomenon.

Puerto Rico is facing the challenge of an aging population in an unusual manner. The combination of population size, political status, and the economic situation means Puerto Rico is unique. Those elements make it difficult to predict the future of the elders. There is no prior precedent that helps us determine what is going to happen. Avoiding the impact that the constant aging of the population will cause to the majority of the social support systems is not recommendable. There is a need for imminent changes. Puerto Rico has not adapted to the demographic changes, which make crucial changes more difficult to accept and assimilate. The window of opportunity to reform the local systems, and make policy changes, is closing fast. If the inertia continues, the social and financial cost of this phenomenon might be too much to handle.

More Policies, Less Politics

With all the challenges and problems in Puerto Rico, what can be done to mitigate the aging of the population? The first step is that the government must acknowledge the implications of the demographic changes and especially the aging of the population in the future development of Puerto Rico. The colony already has an old age structure, which continues to get older with time. The current and future administrations cannot sit back and watch as society is being destroyed by the demographic changes. They cannot wait until there is a deficit of workers to maintain the economy, or a shortage of health professionals to take care of the community, or a lack of people to take care of elders.

Most of the time, the government has to deal with so many situations, which lead them to operate in a reactive approach, or what is commonly called "putting out the fire." The fundamental problem is that the demographic changes could cause a voracious fire, which will be harder to control than the day-to-day issues. To prevent this fire, the inactivity regarding the demographic changes needs to be one of the first things to change. To be effective, most planning efforts will need to consider the expected demographic transformations. Population changes need to have a higher priority within the government agenda.

Dealing with the imminent challenges caused by the demographic transition will require changes in the way the decisions are made. This will require better statistics, as well as more planning and less improvisation. In other words, Puerto Rico needs more policies and less politics.

Knowing the challenges will assist in the process of developing strategies appropriate for the people of Puerto Rico; strategies that consider all the demographic changes and their implications to society. These policies also need to consider the relationship between Puerto Rico and the United States. Furthermore, some of the possible policies might require the approval and consent of the United States. The colony might receive support from the United States, or other countries in the transition to an older society. Current and future administrations will need to learn about the advantages and disadvantages of dealing with the demographic changes as a colony.

With one of the lowest labor force participation rates in the world, and the lowest among the United States jurisdictions, policies that increase it need to be a priority. The new policies must focus in facilitating the participation in the labor force of older people and women. Since an older workforce will be inevitable, policies that facilitate the permanency and insertion of older people in the workforce are going to be essential. This will require legislation and policies to promote and protect the rights of the elder people in the workplaces. Barriers that prevent the elders the opportunity to continue working, after a particular age, need to be eliminated. Employers must adapt to the new demographic reality. Furthermore, employers will need to develop options for this group, in term of better training opportunities, flexible work-times, part-times jobs, and better workplace designs. The negative perceptions that old people are less productive need to change, in order for these possible policies to succeed. With fewer workers and an older population, Puerto Rico will have to rely more on a productive population to break out of the recession and maintain a sustainable economy. This will be impossible if the current labor force participation persist for a significant time. Society cannot expect that fewer workers continue to generate the indispensable national product to maintain the entire population.

Women are the other group that could be more active in the workforce. Currently, women are not treated equally in the labor market. The lack of childcare options in Puerto Rico means that women interested in having child are forced to make significant sacrifices. Most of the time, women are forced to limit their working careers or make drastic changes in order to accommodate their children's necessities. Providing good quality and affordable alternative for the care of children, and developing policies that ease the permanence of women with a child in their work, are going to be crucial to boost females' labor force participation. Promoting flexible work arrangements could be an effective way to increase labor force participation for this group. Considering that, in July 2013, only 33% of the women 15 years of age or more were working or looking for work,[51] the government should have a goal to increase the number of women who are active in the labor force.

-----

[51] Puerto Rico Department of Labor and Human Resource, Working Group Survey, July 2013. Retrieved from http://www.trabajo.pr.gov

Policies to increase the labor force participation of elders and women will benefit the economy, but emigration will continue to be one of the main causes of the drop in the labor force participation and the number of workers on the island. Puerto Rico cannot allow losing more of its working population. For the economy to improve, the country requires every skilled body. The dilemma is that the island is competing with other countries in the world for the best talent, and Puerto Ricans are very talented. Many aspects of society need to improve in order to retain the talent, and to maintain competitiveness. In the previous chapters, I explained the main reasons for the mass exodus from Puerto Rico. Further efforts should be made, in order to improve the investment climate and the design of a new tax system that encourage people to work. Each year the cost of doing business in Puerto Rico is increasing, and the current tax system stimulates emigration and dependency.

In addition to the economic circumstances, few people can tolerate the crime rates and the violence levels of Puerto Rico. The quality of life in Puerto Rico is deplorable, and recent opinion surveys indicate that people do not feel safe. That is why dealing with the pushing factors is essential. Not dealing with the pushing factors will guarantee more emigration and fewer people working in the future.

In many aspects, education will be a key determinant to the future of Puerto Rico. Improving education could help in the process of dealing with many of the pushing factors. A better educated society should be less violent and more prepare for the ever changing workplace. The people expect too much of the youthful population of Puerto Rico, but the education system is not helping this group to fully achieve their potential. The current educational infrastructure requires a drastic transformation to develop a more productive and adaptable workforce in the future. Puerto Rico will fail to compete with other countries if the education system continues to focus teaching students to memorize facts.

The education systems, including tertiary education institutions, need to identify the requirements of the business community. A good education system will be able to recognize what employers in Puerto Rico and around the world expect from workers. Otherwise, universities will continue to produce thousands of professionals with degrees with little or no demand in Puerto Rico. These professionals have limited options, therefore, pushing them to emigrate. For this reason, any adjustment to the education systems will require stronger interactions with the labor markets to be effective.

The country's economy also depends on their people's education. Not only does Puerto Rico call for better learning outcome from their education systems, the aging of the population will require lifelong learning opportunities for the adult population. The changes in the population and technology will require continuous retraining, and better education where people will be able to retrain. Technology changes will force companies to invest in education for their employees to preserve competitiveness. The changes to the education system in the future will dictate the capacity of future generations to adapt to changes in the work environment and take advantage of new opportunities.

Changes to the retirement systems are imminent, but the situation is complicated. The options to transform a defined benefit retirement system, like the one for teachers, are limited. The system will probably change to a defined contribution retirement system for future generations, but not before one or more of the following changes are implemented to the system:

- •Increase in the retirement age.
- •Increase in taxes to people or corporations.
- •Increase in the workers' contributions to the retirement plan.
- •Reduction of benefits for current or future retirees.

The primary decision from the government is who is going to pay and suffer the consequence of waiting too long to reform. They could opt for a combination of alternatives and distribute the burden between the retired people and workers or they could take the decision to throw the burden to future generations. Because of the high political cost, it is unlikely a reduction of benefits will happen to current retirees. Future generations of retirees will be considered less vulnerable than the elders and more capable of assimilating the changes of the system reform.

Regardless of the path taken to reform, it is not going to be a pleasant one. Changes in the retirement plan could increase the economic vulnerability of future generations, especially for teachers who do not contribute to the Social Security system. After all the changes to the retirement systems, there are no guarantees of protection against the loss of income at advanced ages.

The population of Puerto Rico will continue to shrink and get older. Besides that, the future is uncertain. The interaction between the demographic components and the economy is complex, with one affecting the other at any given moment. Especially important will be the fiscal situation and the possibility of a credit downgrade to junk status. There is also the fact that the people of Puerto Rico do not have complete control over their political status and their future. A change of status could have a considerable effect for the demographic dynamics of the island.

While the government must recognize the scope of the new demographic reality and adjust their policies, the people need to acknowledge that some of the adjustment will be painful and unpopular. They also need to be aware that, in the future, most of them would have to remain in the workforce and work for a longer time.

Following decades of pleasing and making popular decisions, the moment for taking the difficult ones has arrived. Regardless of the changes that might occur, the government needs to ensure that the rights of the elders are respected. At the end, the prime challenge for Puerto Rico does not come from its demography, but from the inability of society and their leaders to deal with it.

About the Author

Raúl Figueroa Rodríguez studied a Bachelor's degree in General Science at the University of Puerto Rico, Río Piedras campus. He holds a master degree in Science in Demography, from the University of Puerto Rico, Medical Sciences Campus. Raúl has several publications in academic journals and media on various demographic topics. He is working as an adviser in demographic and statistical issues for various private and public entities. He is the co-author of the book Puerto Rico 2000-2010: Más Allá del Censo [Puerto Rico 2000-2010: Beyond the Census].

Email: demografia.puertorico@gmail.com
Twitter: @rafigueroa

Cover art by: Edwin Pérez-Caraballo
Email: edwinperezcaraballo@yahoo.com

www.ingramcontent.com/pod-product-compliance
Lightning Source LLC
Chambersburg PA
CBHW070324290526
45791CB00003B/1243